●═ MEASURING TEAM PERFORMANCE

A Practical Guide To Tracking Team Success

Gloria E. Bader

Audrey E. Bloom

Richard Y. Chang

KOGAN PAGE

First published in 1994 by Richard Chang Associates, Inc., USA.

This edition published in 1995 by Kogan Page Ltd.

Kogan Page Limited
120 Pentonville Road
London N1 9JN

© 1994, Richard Chang Associates, Inc., 41 Corporate Park, Suite 230, Irvine, CA 92714 USA.

British Library Cataloguing in Publication Data

A CIP record for this book is available from the British Library.

ISBN 0 7494 1662 9

Printed and bound in Great Britain by
Biddles Ltd, Guildford and King's Lynn

ACKNOWLEDGMENTS

About The Authors

Gloria E. Bader is President of The Bader Group, a San Diego-based management consulting firm specializing in leadership, communication, customer service, and teamwork. She is a popular lecturer at San Diego State University's School of Business and an executive coach at the Center for Creative Leadership.

Audrey E. Bloom is a freelance instructional designer with a Masters degree in Educational Technology from San Diego State University. She researches and develops training materials on a wide range of technical and management topics.

Richard Y. Chang is President and CEO of Richard Chang Associates, Inc., a diversified organizational improvement consulting firm based in Irvine, California. He is internationally recognized and highly respected for his management strategy, quality improvement, organization development, customer satisfaction, and human resource development expertise.

The authors would like to acknowledge the support of the entire team of professionals at Richard Chang Associates, Inc. for their contribution to the guidebook development process. In addition, special thanks are extended to the many client organizations who have helped us shape the practical ideas and proven methods shared in this guidebook.

Additional Credits

Editor:	Sarah Ortlieb Fraser
Reviewer:	P. Keith Kelly
Graphic Layout:	Christina Slater and Dottie Snyder
Cover Design:	John Odam Design Associates

PREFACE

The 1990's have already presented individuals and organizations with some very difficult challenges to face and overcome. So who will have the advantage as we move toward the year 2000 and beyond?

The advantage will belong to those with a commitment to continuous learning. Whether on an individual basis or as an entire organization, one key ingredient to building a continuous learning environment is *The Practical Guidebook Collection* brought to you by the Publications Division of Richard Chang Associates, Inc.

After understanding the future *"learning needs"* expressed by our clients and other potential customers, we are pleased to publish *The Practical Guidebook Collection*. These guidebooks are designed to provide you with proven, *"real-world"* tips, tools, and techniques— on a wide range of subjects—that you can apply in the workplace and/or on a personal level immediately.

Once you've had a chance to benefit from *The Practical Guidebook Collection*, please share your feedback with us. We've included a brief *Evaluation and Feedback Form* at the end of the guidebook that you can fax to us.

With your feedback, we can continuously improve the resources we are providing through the Publications Division of Richard Chang Associates, Inc.

Wishing you successful reading,

Richard Y. Chang
President and CEO
Richard Chang Associates, Inc.

TABLE OF CONTENTS

A student pilot was on his first solo flight. When he called in for instructions, someone in the control tower said, *"Would you please give your altitude and position?"*

The pilot said, *"I'm 5 feet 10 inches, and I'm sitting up front."*

The moral of this story:
Make sure the measurements you are collecting are really the ones you need.

CHAPTER ONE

INTRODUCTION

Why Read This Guidebook?

As organizations flatten or streamline from many layers of bosses to team structures, team leaders and members find that they must perform many management duties. They need to learn about problem-solving techniques, data collection methods, and meeting effectiveness. These changes also call for new ways to measure performance. Teams rarely know how to check their own strengths and evaluate their skills.

For example, a few years ago, Trina received an annual performance review about her work as a receptionist in a busy outpatient department. She was evaluated on her efficiency, customer service, and communication skills by her supervisor (*who rarely observed her work*). Although she performs the same receptionist duties as before, Trina is now part of an eight-person office team that meets weekly to solve problems, improve customer service and quality, and measure their own effectiveness.

Measuring the effectiveness of a team such as Trina's, that sets goals, assigns duties, and schedules its own work, calls for a different mindset and new tools. Traditional methods of performance measurement simply do not work.

Measuring Team Performance provides practical methods for teams to evaluate their performance, dynamics, and effectiveness.

Who Should Read This Guidebook?

Team leaders and members of new teams, task forces, and well-established teams will find these tools and examples valuable. Project teams with special goals and short time frames, as well as committees and quality-improvement teams, all require periodic measurement. If a team is defined as a group of people working toward a common goal, then even the group that plans your organization's holiday party can benefit from the ideas in this guidebook.

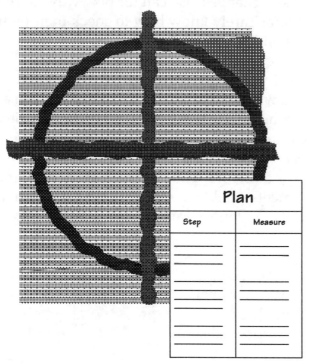

Measurement is essential at every stage of a team's development. Measuring effectiveness can even motivate a team that needs a charge of new energy. Team facilitators or trainers responsible for building teams can and should employ these tools. Managers or human resource professionals who develop organizational incentive and reward systems will find practical suggestions here for improving team reward and compensation.

When And How To Use It

Ideally, goals and measures are set when a team forms or begins a new task. *Measuring Team Performance* provides suggestions for defining the goals and determining the measures that new teams need. Using this guidebook, teams can agree on types and frequency of measures and conduct their baseline *(or first time)* measures.

Sometimes teams form spontaneously to meet the needs of an immediate business crisis. In such cases, the last thing on the team's collective mind is measurement. Even teams formed in this way can develop a measurement system to use from that point forward. It is never too late to begin measuring a team's effectiveness. This guidebook's tools and techniques apply at any stage of a team's development.

Use this guidebook to design measurement tools that fit your special circumstance. Some tools work better in certain situations; others take more time to implement. Each tool that follows *(survey, observation, interviews, critical incidents, and existing data)* is explained so that you will know when to use it, how to administer it, and how to summarize and use the results. You will find examples and design suggestions for each tool.

Before you begin, you must believe in the value of measurement. The next chapter should convince you!

WHY MEASURE?

"What gets measured gets done."

Tom Peters

Successful teams are committed to results. They frequently seek feedback on their performance and respond to their findings with action. Tracking a team's progress toward one or more business goals for product and service quality is the primary reason for measurement. Other benefits include improving effectiveness as a team, building motivation, and rewarding performance.

Product And Service Quality

There is no doubt that the essential work of teams is to achieve and even exceed business goals for sales, productivity, quality and customer service. These products and services are the building blocks of any organization's success. Most organizations will want concrete proof of their teams' impact on each or any of these factors.

This guidebook looks at three teams—Trina's Outpatient Department Team, Mike's New Product Development Team, and Lee's Hotel Registration Desk Team. Following are examples of their respective goals *(each of which are measurable)*.

➤ Reduce the patient check-in and waiting time by 50 percent while maintaining a 90 percent rating on customer satisfaction *(an example of service quality)*.

➤ Design and fabricate a prototype of the new collapsible ski pole by June 1st with 100 percent accordance to specifications and within budget *(an example of product quality)*.

➤ Increase repeat guest business from 10 to 15 percent of total registrations while improving the coordination between the hotel registration desk and the sales department *(an example of service quality)*.

Each of these measures requires a baseline measurement of some kind. A baseline is a starting point. It is a measure of *"where we are now."* For example, if you want to lose ten pounds, you must know what you weigh at the start of your diet.

Let's look at Trina's Outpatient Department Team. To measure progress against their objective, the team must know the current registration time—they must conduct a baseline measurement. After a certain period of time, the team's improvements will appear in a follow-up measurement. Time saved usually means money saved; in this case, it also means better customer service for patients. This is sound business practice.

Effectiveness As A Team

Teams must also know how to measure their effectiveness in working together. Do they communicate with one another? How well do they diagnose and solve problems? Does each member understand his or her role on the team? Consider a team like Trina's, solving daily problems in the outpatient department office. Perhaps there is a new receptionist who does not know his duties; or the data entry clerk forgets to tell the doctor that she needed to sign an insurance form. When mistakes occur and things fall apart, the causes and solutions are often found within the team.

How the team reaches or exceeds its business goals depends upon the team's dynamics. Team dynamics include roles, responsibilities, and clear guidelines. It also involves the interpersonal communication skills of its members—how they talk, listen, cooperate, and coordinate with one another.

On the basis of their goals and stages of development, teams need to measure any number of these factors:

- Clarity of goals and objectives

- Achievement of results

- Structure

- Problem-solving skills

- Support of leadership

- Use of team resources

- Recognition and motivation

- Conflict management

- Understanding of roles

- Effectiveness of communication

- Creativity

Motivation

Most people want to know how they are doing. Little or no feedback is frustrating and demotivating, leading individuals and teams to wonder, *"Has anyone noticed?"* Measures give clear feedback. A team that measures its effectiveness, sees its progress, and discovers and implements improvements will strengthen its own commitment and energy. Success encourages more success.

Compensation And Rewards

Many organizations have created reward systems for both teams and individuals. Therefore, every team must know how to measure its business results. The team's performance may influence the salaries, bonuses, and other incentives for everyone on the team.

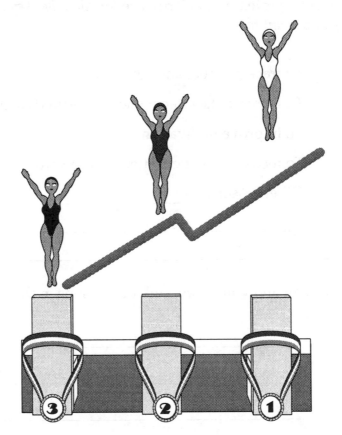

Teams flourish in environments where there is a direct relationship between results and rewards. Good measurements, drawn from a variety of sources, provide objective evidence that is difficult to ignore.

Now that you and your team believe in the importance of measurement, how do you begin?

CHAPTER TWO WORKSHEET: WHY MEASURE YOUR TEAM?

1. With your team, rank in order of importance *(1 = most important, 2 = next most, etc.)* the following possible reasons for measuring your team's performance *(or add other key reasons that may be important to your team).*

    ____ To track product and service quality

    ____ To increase the effectiveness of team dynamics

    ____ To improve motivation

    ____ To focus on compensation and rewards

    ____ Other reasons: _____

    ____ _____

    ____ _____

2. Why did you and your team rank the reasons in this order?

    _____

    _____

    _____

    _____

    _____

    _____

    _____

    _____

3. Do you think these reasons will be changing as your team
    evolves or as its mission *(purpose)* changes over the short-term?
    The long-term?

    _____

    _____

    _____

    _____

    _____

    _____

4. What obstacles are there *(existing or potential)* to effectively
    measuring your team's performance?

    _____

    _____

    _____

    _____

    _____

    _____

    _____

    _____

GETTING STARTED

"Without measurement, you are aiming at nothing and will surely hit it."
Source unknown

The Decision To Measure

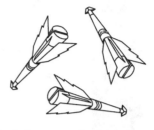

Think about it. Most school children would rejoice if report cards were completely eliminated, yet most parents want to know how their children are progressing in their classes. Sunday afternoon football would lose much of its appeal if the football coaches decided they no longer needed to keep score, or could not agree how.

When establishing business measurements, your team must establish some ground rules. Before you draft the first survey or interview form, each team member must understand the purpose and framework of your measurement tools.

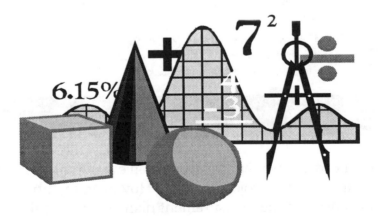

You should know that there are pitfalls to avoid when measuring team performance. Some teams measure everything in sight. They drown in numbers and reports. Other teams measure factors that are not relevant to their goals.

As you and your teammates decide and plan to measure, try to agree on your approach by checking off these points together:

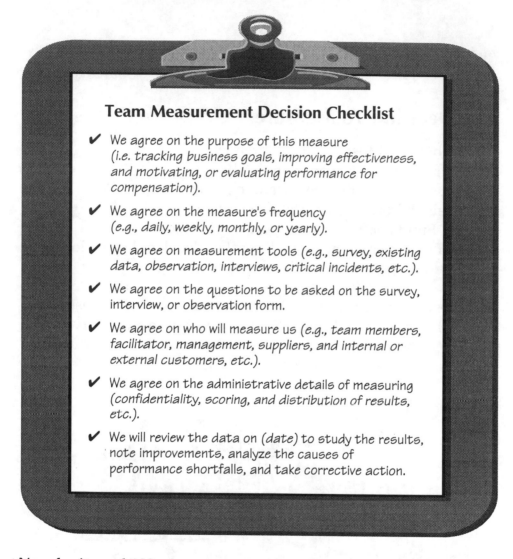

Team Measurement Decision Checklist

✔ We agree on the purpose of this measure (i.e. tracking business goals, improving effectiveness, and motivating, or evaluating performance for compensation).

✔ We agree on the measure's frequency (e.g., daily, weekly, monthly, or yearly).

✔ We agree on measurement tools (e.g., survey, existing data, observation, interviews, critical incidents, etc.).

✔ We agree on the questions to be asked on the survey, interview, or observation form.

✔ We agree on who will measure us (e.g., team members, facilitator, management, suppliers, and internal or external customers, etc.).

✔ We agree on the administrative details of measuring (confidentiality, scoring, and distribution of results, etc.).

✔ We will review the data on (date) to study the results, note improvements, analyze the causes of performance shortfalls, and take corrective action.

You don't need 100 percent agreement on every point. That would become a major team project in itself. However, members need to reach consensus on the measurement plan and assure that everyone on the team can live with the decisions. You can use a matrix like the one illustrated in Chapter Four, Team Measurement Planning Worksheet, to plot your ideas (*see the Appendix for a blank worksheet you may copy and use*).

What To Measure?

Often, the number one reason to measure is to track the progress and completion of your team's business objective(s). Some objectives (*e.g., to complete all insurance forms by the last day of the month*) remain constant. Other objectives are likely to change over time. An example of a short-term objective would be: train office managers to use the new index as they complete the forms. Changing objectives need new measures.

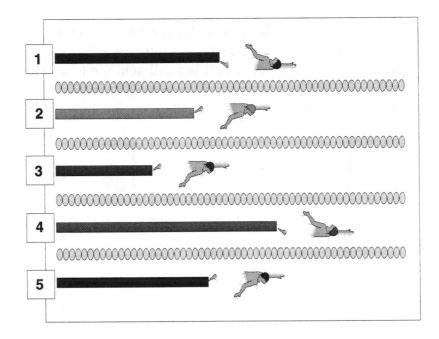

It's best to measure the progress toward your business goals and your team's effectiveness at the same time. Therefore, your team must measure its own dynamics and communication.

Many teams make the mistake of waiting until the end of the year or until a project is completed before they evaluate their own dynamics and communication. At that point, it is disheartening and unproductive to realize that roles were not clear or that misunderstandings existed.

The primary focus of Trina and her team was . . .
measuring the quality of their services. They decided to break this overall measure into several smaller measures. As they had discovered during a brainstorming session, it was easy to fall into the trap of measuring things that were not absolutely necessary. The team agreed that for a measure to be included, they had to be able to answer *"yes"* to the question, *"Does this measure give us critical information about our team's performance?"* . . .

Who Should Measure?

Teams that consult multiple sources for information on their performance and effectiveness receive powerful and objective feedback. By soliciting and using this feedback, the team is involving others in the measurement process. Valuable sources of feedback data for teams include:

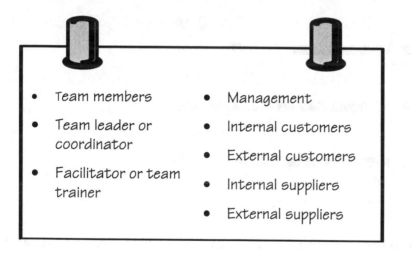

- Team members
- Team leader or coordinator
- Facilitator or team trainer

- Management
- Internal customers
- External customers
- Internal suppliers
- External suppliers

Trina and Sandra . . .
the data entry clerk, track the percentage of late insurance claims, and the total number of new and existing patients. Trina also records notes about difficult patient registration incidents. . . .

☤ *On a monthly basis . . .*

Trina's entire team uses a Team Success Survey *(or self-assessment)*, illustrated in Chapter Five. The results of this survey help the team discuss conflicts and reduce misunderstandings. . . .

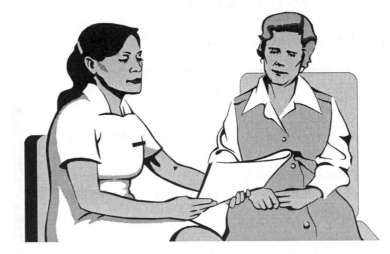

☤ *Trina's department solicits feedback . . .*

from patients and insurance companies *(external customers)*, as well as nurses and physicians *(internal customers)*. Six months from now, her team plans to broaden their sources to include management and the admissions department *(internal suppliers)*, as well as their three largest medical suppliers *(external suppliers)*. . . .

When To Measure?

There are no set formulas for when to measure. Key criteria include how you intend to use the data, the human effort required to collect the information, and the maturity of the team. Newer teams measure more frequently than experienced teams.

Teams can measure at the start and conclusion of projects, during projects, weekly, monthly, quarterly, or yearly. When working with large volumes of product or service outputs, teams often find a great deal of value in daily data collection.

The first data you collect is your baseline measurement and you will compare all other measures to that.

Here are a few general guidelines:

➠ Measure in time to take corrective action.

➠ Measure subgoals, milestones, or completed steps toward accomplishment of your team's goals.

➠ Measure in time for regular performance reviews.

➠ Measure ongoing teamwork factors, such as meeting effectiveness, communication, and conflict resolution.

➠ Save time and duplication of your measurement efforts by using existing data such as your organization's annual employee opinion survey or customer service information.

At first, it might seem that implementing these suggestions about what, who, and when to measure requires extraordinary analytical skills. That's not so! Through experimentation, high-performance teams learn to streamline their measurements. They keep their data collection simple by replacing or refining unsuccessful measures.

Trina's team decided . . .

that they needed to track different measures at different intervals. Specifically, they decided to track late insurance claims monthly and monitor the number of total and new patients daily. The team chose to record incidents as they occur, to avoid losing or forgetting good information. Now the team compiles and uses all of their information during their weekly meetings.

CHAPTER THREE WORKSHEET:
ESTABLISHING THE GROUNDWORK

1. Use the Team Measurement Decision Checklist *(see the Appendix)* to facilitate discussion and a team decision on the issues relating to team measurement. What additional issues should be part of your decision?

_____

_____

_____

_____

_____

_____

2. What will your team measure?

_____

_____

_____

_____

_____

_____

_____

3. Who will gather the measurement data and who will provide input?

_____

_____

_____

_____

_____

_____

_____

4. When will the information be gathered? When will it be reviewed?

_____

_____

_____

_____

_____

_____

_____

MEET THE TEAMS

As mentioned in Chapter Two, this guidebook looks at three teams:

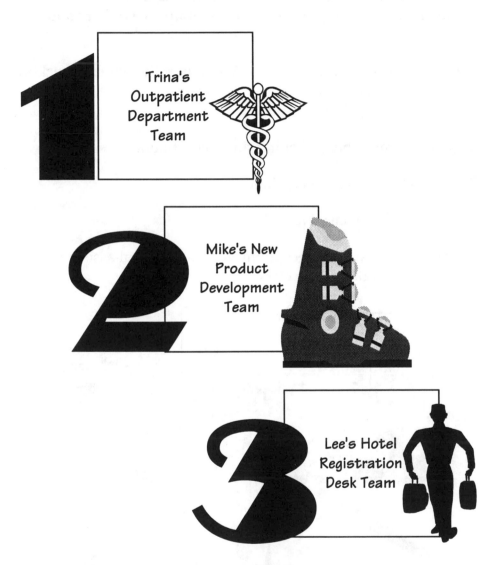

1 Trina's Outpatient Department Team

2 Mike's New Product Development Team

3 Lee's Hotel Registration Desk Team

You've already encountered Trina's Outpatient Department team. Now you'll learn more about all three teams. In this chapter you'll also find Team Measurement Planning Worksheets for each team, which outline each team's plans to measure its performance.

⚕ Trina's Outpatient Department Team

Mission: We support the hospital's mission to exceed patient expectations in a cost-effective and caring manner. Our department seeks ways to continuously improve quality and customer service.

Current business objective: We will reduce the patient check-in and waiting time by 50 percent while maintaining a 90 percent rating on customer satisfaction.

Type of team: A busy evening shift department

Team leader: Trina, a receptionist

Experience on teams: New

Seven members: Two receptionists, three medical assistants, one nurse, and one data entry clerk

TEAM MEASUREMENT PLANNING WORKSHEET:
OUTPATIENT DEPARTMENT TEAM

Teams Business Objective: Reduce patient waiting time by 50% in the Outpatient Department.

Note: ▲ Denotes a possible key measure for performance evaluation.

— Denotes that this type of measure does not apply in this case.

TYPE OF MEASURE	WHO TO CONDUCT	SOURCES	TIMES/ FREQUENCY	NOTES
Existing data		The Employee Opinion Survey produced lower than expected marks on "Cooperation and Communication" Hospital's Patient Satisfaction Survey also pointed to problems with outpatient waiting times		▲ Future Opinion Surveys could be used as measures for performance evaluations ▲ Future patient Satisfaction Surveys could be used as measures
Critical incidents		Angry patient's letter received Physician's phone call and memo to hospital administration		
Observation	Team trainer from Human Resources, or other Human Resources personnel	Observe in waiting area and treatment rooms	45 min. sessions 2X per day for one week	▲ Check sheet to record patient waiting times (from arrival to start of treatment) Want extensive qualitative info on staff interactions
Survey	Human Resources assistance needed			Team Success Survey strongly recommended on a monthly basis Add in-depth questions on trust and communication for targeted improvement
Interviews	—	—	—	—
Phone survey or interview	—	—	—	—

Mike's New Product Development Team

Mission: We shall design and engineer new products that will rapidly and efficiently increase our sales and customer satisfaction.

Current business objective: We will design and fabricate a prototype of the new collapsible ski pole by June 1st with 100 percent accordance to specification and within budget.

Type of team: Cross-functional, fast-response project team *(engineering, sales, manufacturing, and purchasing)*

Team leader: Mike, an engineer

Experience on teams: All members experienced on other project teams

Seven members: Two engineers, one materials technician, one sales representative, two manufacturing technicians, and one metals supplier

TEAM MEASUREMENT PLANNING WORKSHEET: NEW PRODUCT DEVELOPMENT TEAM

Teams Business Objective: Design, develop and prepare a prototype collapsible ski pole for manufacturing within 90 days.

Note: ▲ Denotes a possible key measure for performance evaluation.
— Denotes that this type of measure does not apply in this case.

TYPE OF MEASURE	WHO TO CONDUCT	SOURCES	TIMES/ FREQUENCY	NOTES
Existing data		Planning and milestone charts from previous new product team, and from first four weeks of this team's work		▲ Organization-wide Employee Opinion Survey (see survey notes on engineering communication with customers)
Critical incidents	—	—	—	—
Observation	—	—	—	—
Survey	Brenda's intern to develop/send/ collect	Minimum six internal customers; possibly outside suppliers	(2x) Review at mid-project and repeat at project end	▲ Use short peer review feedback survey Brenda to summarize and provide feedback
Interviews	Brenda from Personnel to conduct approximately 10 to 12 interviews	Mike's team Previous new product team	One time only May repeat in future to support cross-functional team development	Short, 5-item interview (approx. 20 minutes each) Brenda to summarize and provide feedback on individual basis
Phone survey or interview	—	—	—	—

Lee's Hotel Registration Desk Team

Mission: We will build loyal customers through friendly and efficient guest services in the mid-price range.

Current business objective: We will seek to increase repeat business from 10 to 15 percent of total registrations while improving the coordination between the hotel registration desk and the sales department.

Type of team: Continuous quality and service improvement

Team Leader: Lee, a senior front-desk clerk

Experience on teams: Two years

Six members: Three front-desk clerks from different shifts of a 500-room hotel, and three sales representatives

TEAM MEASUREMENT PLANNING WORKSHEET:
HOTEL REGISTRATION TEAM

Teams Business Objective: Increase guest return rate from 10% to 15%.

Note: ▲ Denotes a possible key measure for performance evaluation.
— Denotes that this type of measure does not apply in this case.

TYPE OF MEASURE	WHO TO CONDUCT	SOURCES	TIMES/ FREQUENCY	NOTES
Existing data	Team leader summarizes, presents in next team meeting	Industry averages from trade publications Hotel computer records of registered guests	Use last quarter's data, update each quarter	IMPORTANT: Request Information Systems to prepare printouts that sort registration information by new guests and returning guests
Critical incidents	—	—	—	—
Observation	Marketing assistant to observe registrations Catering manager to observe checkout procedures	Observe staff at registration area	(3X) 30-minute sessions X2 days Friday and Saturday or Thursday and Friday	Registration staff team will not be shown the registration check sheet in advance
Survey	Self-administered	Registration team members; all shifts	Repeat after 6 weeks, then at 3 months, then at 6 months	Team Success Survey
Interviews	—	—	—	—
Phone survey or interview	Calls to be made by regular staff or marketing staff	Hotel guests who have departed within the last 24 hours. Every fourth guest in register will be called (25% sample)	Daily for 2 weeks Possibly repeat as needed after 6 months	▲ Consider for use in performance evaluations if repeated after 6 months

CHAPTER FOUR WORKSHEET: PLANNING FOR TEAM PERFORMANCE MEASUREMENT

1. What is your team's mission?

_____

_____

_____

_____

_____

_____

2. What is your team's business objective?

_____

_____

_____

_____

_____

_____

_____

_____

3. As a team, complete a Team Measurement Planning Worksheet. List key questions or concerns you need to address.

   Note: You may copy and use the blank worksheet in Appendix B or create your own.

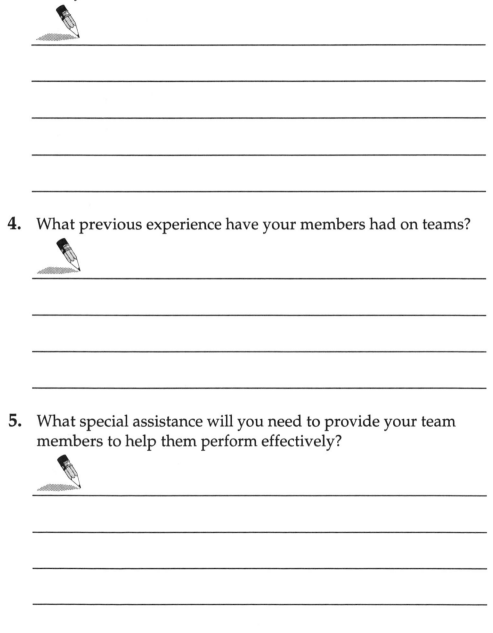

   _____

   _____

   _____

   _____

   _____

4. What previous experience have your members had on teams?

   _____

   _____

   _____

   _____

5. What special assistance will you need to provide your team members to help them perform effectively?

   _____

   _____

   _____

   _____

   _____

QUANTITATIVE MEASURES: THE POWER OF NUMBERS

Collecting The Data

Quantitative measures are the numbers of performance. They include such things as total units produced, dollars earned, percentage increases or decreases, ratios of product produced to resources required, and average times. These numbers allow you to easily compare where the team is now to where it was six months ago, or to where it wants to be six months in the future. Numbers also allow teams and organizations to compare where they are relative to industry averages.

Measurement data provides teams and their organizations with information about progress and results (*e.g., the reduction in rework hours and costs, or the increase in customer satisfaction over the last quarter*). Quantitative measures are clear, compact, and direct. In many organizations, numbers also drive bonuses and rewards.

In short, numbers are powerful.

⇟ *Via computer, Lee's department . . .*

continuously counts the number of hotel guests registered. They use this number in the baseline calculation of return guests. The current guest return rate is 10 percent.

Although the 10 percent figure gives Lee's team some information, the number does not tell them why guests return, nor, more importantly, does it provide information about the 90 percent who do not return. . . .

You and your team can discover such answers by collecting qualitative measures. Qualitative measures reveal the explanations, feelings, and reasons behind the numbers. Both quantitative and qualitative measures are necessary when teams measure their performance.

QUANTITATIVE TOOLS	QUALITATIVE TOOLS
Surveys	Interviews
Observation	Observation
Existing Data	Critical Incidents

There are several primary methods teams use to collect quantitative data, and hundreds of variations on those basic tools. In the following pages, you will learn about three of them: Surveys, Observation, and Existing Data.

Sometimes called questionnaires, surveys are used to quickly gather data from small or large groups of people. Surveys can tell you about customer attitudes and opinions and help you gain insight into the internal workings of a group.

Developing Surveys

To successfully gather team performance information, you must develop a survey that provides the *"right"* information, is objective, easy to use, and simple to analyze. To develop such a survey you first need to consider the following guidelines: elements of a survey, creating appropriate scales, and using open-ended questions.

THE ELEMENTS OF A SURVEY

A simple, personalized cover letter
The cover letter or opening paragraph of the survey contains a short explanation of the survey's purpose, use of the data, and commitment to confidentiality.

Directions
Explain how to complete the survey and include the required return date.

Objective items
Survey questions are called items. Avoid using any more items than necessary. Each item should relate to the survey's purpose. Include more interesting items at the beginning to gain the survey participant's attention.

Open-ended items
Open-ended items give people a chance to add anything else they might have on their minds, or to expand on an earlier item.

Demographic items
If you need information about the survey participants, include these items at the end of the survey. Keep these questions brief and focused on your survey's goal.

Rating scales
Scales make it easy to rank answers from low to high. It's best to use five to seven choices. Make sure the scales you choose match the items you are using.

It's also important to label scales correctly. For example, if the information you are seeking has to do with time, use words such as *"Always, Often, Sometimes,"* etc. Response scales that ask people for their level of agreement with a statement *(using terms such as "Strongly Agree, Agree, Neutral," etc.)* are familiar and easy to use.

Lastly, it's best not to mix scales on a survey. If you are using more than one scale, make sure the respondent can see the difference.

Creating appropriate scales

Begin by thinking in the most simple way about what you want to measure. Is it frequency, speed, quality, agreement, or effectiveness? Then think about descriptors for a range of that measure, moving from low to high. For example, consider terms such as *"Never to Always, Strongly Disagree to Strongly Agree,"* etc.

Place the highest and lowest descriptors at either end of your scale, and identify terms that would complete the positions between the two ends. Use at least five positions; seven or nine if you need more precision in the responses.

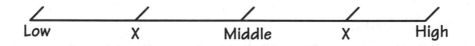

Low   X   Middle   X   High

Finally, make sure you word your questions so that the selections on the scale fit the questions or statements.

Several sets of scales follow, along with sample questions that you might use with them. Generally you would list the questions, with scales following each.

Note: The choices *"Do Not Know"* and *"Does Not Apply"* are typically included, but are not considered part of a numerical scale.

Question: To what degree do you agree with the following statements?

Using a five-point scale:

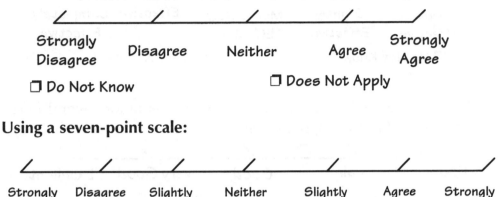

Strongly Disagree   Disagree   Neither   Agree   Strongly Agree

☐ Do Not Know   ☐ Does Not Apply

Using a seven-point scale:

Strongly Disagree   Disagree   Slightly Disagree   Neither Agree nor Disagree   Slightly Agree   Agree   Strongly Agree

☐ Do Not Know   ☐ Does Not Apply

Question: How often do members of your group do (something), say (something), etc.? (*You would list the behaviors, with a scale after each.*)

Using a five-point scale:

Never   Seldom   Occasionally   Often   Always

☐ Do Not Know   ☐ Does Not Apply

Question: To what extent are the following customer service problems evident in your organization? (*You would list the problems with a scale after each.*)

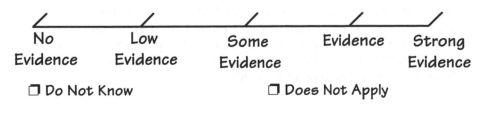

No Evidence   Low Evidence   Some Evidence   Evidence   Strong Evidence

☐ Do Not Know   ☐ Does Not Apply

Question: How effective is your team's leader with respect to the following skills? *(List the skills you want to measure, with a scale after each.)*

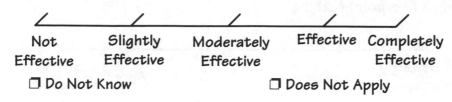

Not   Slightly   Moderately   Effective   Completely
Effective   Effective   Effective   Effective

☐ Do Not Know   ☐ Does Not Apply

Question: How would you rate today's presentation, overall? *(You could also list various aspects of the presentation, with a scale after each.)*

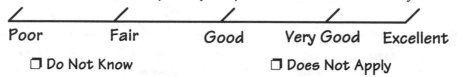

Poor   Fair   Good   Very Good   Excellent

☐ Do Not Know   ☐ Does Not Apply

Coding

Decide in advance how to average and graph the survey responses. For example, are *"Strongly Agree"* responses counted as seven points and the *"Slightly Disagree"* responses scored as three points? How will you report the data so that it makes sense to your team? Summary tables and bar charts are two common methods of data presentation.

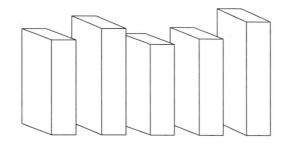

Note: The most useful step you can take in developing surveys is to conduct a trial run or *"pilot"* test. You should even do this for surveys that you will only use once, or distribute to fewer than 50 people. The pilot survey will reveal instructions and items that are not clear, scales that don't make sense, and coding problems you may not have anticipated.

Open-ended questions

Most surveys end with one or two open-ended questions. Open-ended questions give people the opportunity to share thoughts and opinions in their own words.

Here are some examples of open-ended questions:

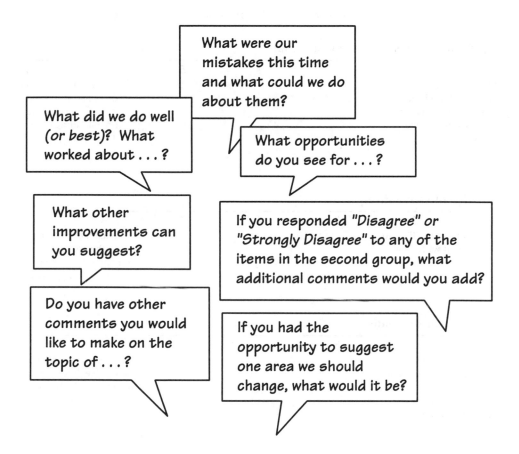

Our teams found these three surveys valuable:

➡ Team Success Survey

➡ Meeting Effectiveness Survey

➡ Peer Feedback Survey

Team Success Survey

↓ *As an experienced work group . . .*

Lee's registration desk staff knows the benefits of periodically evaluating their own team skills. They agreed to retake the Team Success Survey every six months. At today's monthly meeting, each member will complete the twelve-item survey to evaluate their last six months. . . .

Please circle the number on each scale that best describes your perception.

1. Clearly states its mission and goals

1	2	3	4	5	6	7

Team activities demonstrate a lack of focus or understanding of the team's mission and goals.

Team activities demonstrate a clear focus and understanding of the team's mission and goals.

2. Operates creatively

1	2	3	4	5	6	7

The team is unwilling to experiment with new ideas or methods.

The team experiments with new ideas and demonstrates a creative approach.

3. Focuses on results

1	2	3	4	5	6	7

The team does not accomplish its objectives within budget, on schedule, or to the required level of quality.

The team accomplishes its objectives within budget, on schedule and to the required level of quality.

4. Clarifies roles and responsibilities

1	2	3	4	5	6	7

Roles and responsibilities of team members are uncertain.

Roles and responsibilities are clear. Each team member understands what is expected of him or her.

5. Is well-organized

1	2	3	4	5	6	7
The team's structure, policies and procedures are disorganized.					The team's structure, policies, and procedures are defined and supported by its members.	

6. Builds upon individual strengths

1	2	3	4	5	6	7
The knowledge, skills and talents of team members are underutilized.					Members' knowledge, skills and talents are put to good use.	

7. Supports leadership and each other

1	2	3	4	5	6	7
The leadership role is always in the hands of one or two members. Others do not support the leadership.					The leadership role is shared among, and supported by, the team.	

8. Develops team climate

1	2	3	4	5	6	7
Team members feel they would be better off working individually.					Team members work together with a high degree of energy and involvement. There is a strong sense of team spirit.	

9. Resolves disagreements

1	2	3	4	5	6	7
Disagreement among team members interferes with productive work.					Members deal with disagreement openly and constructively.	

10. Communicates openly

1	2	3	4	5	6	7
Day-to-day communication among team members is limited and guarded.					Day-to-day communication among team members is frequent, honest, and direct.	

11. Makes objective decisions

| 1 | 2 | 3 | 4 | 5 | 6 | 7 |

Someone solves problems and makes decisions for the team.

The team identifies and solves its own problems, and makes effective decisions through involvement and consensus.

12. Evaluates its own effectiveness

| 1 | 2 | 3 | 4 | 5 | 6 | 7 |

The team does not evaluate its own effectiveness.

The team continuously evaluates the effectiveness of its dynamics, methods, and performance.

Lee's team was glad to see . . .

the improvements in several of their average scores over the past six months. However, they were disappointed that the previously low scores in Focus and Creativity showed only small improvements. They would need a concentrated effort in those two areas to accomplish their team's business objective. . . .

LEE'S TEAM'S RESULTS

ITEM	PREVIOUS POINTS	PREVIOUS RANK	POINT AVERAGE (NEW)	RANK (NEW)	CHANGE IN POINTS
Clearly states its mission/goals	3.8	11	3.9	11	+.1
Operates creatively	3.9	10	4.2	10	+.3
Focuses on results	4.5	8	4.3	9	-.2
Clarifies roles and responsibilities	5.1	5	5.1	5	--
Is well-organized	5.9	2	5.2	4	-.7
Builds upon individual strengths	4.9	6	4.7	7	-.2
Supports leadership/each other	4.1	9	4.6	8	+.5
Develops team climate	4.9	6	4.9	6	--
Resolves disagreements	5.4	4	5.6	2	+.2
Communicates openly	6.0	1	5.9	1	-.1
Makes objective decisions	4.8	7	4.9	6	+.1
Evaluates its own effectiveness	5.5	3	5.6	2	+.1

Meeting Effectiveness Survey

Most teams depend on meetings to accomplish their work.
Because productive meetings are so critical to team success, and
many teams have problems running good meetings, a Meeting
Effectiveness Survey is an essential team measurement tool.

Meeting Effectiveness Survey Items

Purpose: To continuously seek ways to improve the productivity
of team meetings.

Source of Data: Meeting Attendees

Collected By/When: All attendees to complete at every meeting for
a period of one month; thereafter, once per month or at the
discretion of the meeting facilitator.

1. Did participants receive sufficient notice to prepare for this meeting?

0	1	2
No time	Some time	Sufficient time

2. Did the meeting notice or announcement include the purpose and objectives
    of the meeting?

0	1	2
Not indicated	Stated but unclear	Clearly stated

3. Did the meeting begin within three minutes of its scheduled start time?

0	1	2
No	Yes, but we had to start again for late arrivals	Yes

4. Was an agenda for the meeting prepared in advance, or developed at the
    start of the meeting?

0	1	2
No agenda/No stated objectives	Vague agenda and objectives	Specific agenda and clear objectives

5. At the beginning of the meeting, were the agenda *(including time lines for the topics)* and meeting objectives reviewed by the meeting leader or facilitator?

0	1	2
No	Yes, but not covered adequately	Yes

6. Were participants prepared for this meeting?

0	1	2
Not at all prepared	Somewhat prepared	As prepared as possible

7. Were action items and responsibilities clearly defined, then summarized?

0	1	2
Not at all	Some were/Others fuzzy	Yes

8. I would rate the quality of the group's interaction and member participation during this meeting as:

0	1	2
Having very little value	Fair	Very good/Contributed in a major way to effectiveness

9. Did the meeting generally follow the agenda and achieve its intended purpose?

0	1	2
Did not follow agenda	Followed the agenda somewhat	Followed the agenda in a productive manner

10. Did the meeting end within three minutes of its scheduled completion time, or sooner if business was accomplished?

0	1	2
No	No, but within a reasonable time frame	Yes

11. Overall, how did you feel about the investment of your time in this meeting?

0	1	2
Not at all satisfied/Frustrated	Somewhat satisfied	Completely satisfied/Something was accomplished/A good use of my time

Peer Feedback Survey

When you use a tool to collect data from this circle of people, it is called 360-degree feedback. This type of feedback is useful when a team desires a truly honest look at their interactions, effectiveness, and progress or business results. These multiple viewpoints also increase objectivity when you use performance measures in reward and compensation systems.

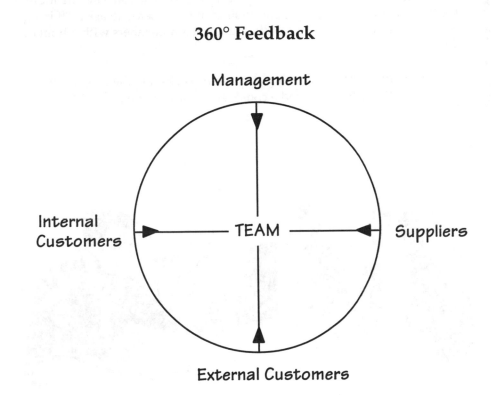

360° Feedback

Let's check on . . .

Mike's New Product Development Team. When an intense, high priority team project like Mike's involves people from a variety of departments or functions for a short period of time *(in this case, only three months)*, every minute counts. Teamwork is critical but sometimes challenging to accomplish.

One of the ground rules set by the team at their first planning meeting was related to the team's need to evaluate their own progress, in terms of project milestones and team dynamics. Some of the team members had valuable experience with peer feedback, the process through which team members ask for and give feedback to one another on their skills and interactions.

Aware of this, Mike's team designed a short peer feedback survey. In addition to the team members evaluating one another, it made sense to ask staff in other departments and suppliers for feedback to the team members with whom they dealt most closely.

At their weekly *"all hands"* meeting about four weeks into the project, the members of Mike's team reached a consensus—they would adopt Mike's survey. . . .

New Product Development Team
Peer Report

For the past month, you have worked closely with

(Name) _____ of the Ski Pole Team.

The feedback from this survey will assist this team member in improving

his/her communication and cooperation with all the departments in our

organization. Our goal is the shortest development cycle and most successful

new product launch in the history of our organization!

Please take a few minutes to complete this survey. Return this form by

Friday, June 5, using the enclosed confidential envelope, to Brenda in Human

Resources. She will tabulate the results and give private feedback to each

team member. No names will appear on the summary. Thank you for your

participation.

Rating Scale

1. Never or Rarely *(less than 10% of the time)*
2. Occasionally *(about 10 to 30% of the time)*
3. Sometimes *(about 30 to 50% of the time)*
4. Frequently *(about 50 to 80% of the time)*
5. Almost always *(more than 80% of the time)*
NA—Does not apply

1. Stays focused on the purpose and goals of the Ski Pole project.

1	2	3	4	5	
Never or Rarely	Occasionally	Sometimes	Frequently	Almost Always	☐ NA

2. Involves you in the data collection process.

1	2	3	4	5	
Never or Rarely	Occasionally	Sometimes	Frequently	Almost Always	☐ NA

3. Delegates tasks when possible; asks for help from others when needed.

1	2	3	4	5	
Never or Rarely	Occasionally	Sometimes	Frequently	Almost Always	☐ NA

4. Learns about your needs and concerns related to the project.

1	2	3	4	5	
Never or Rarely	Occasionally	Sometimes	Frequently	Almost Always	☐ NA

5. Remains open to your suggestions.

1	2	3	4	5	
Never or Rarely	Occasionally	Sometimes	Frequently	Almost Always	☐ NA

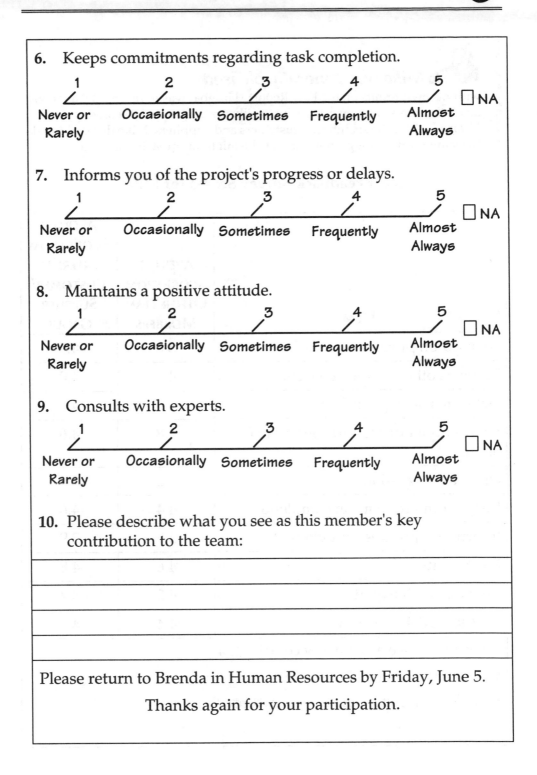

6. Keeps commitments regarding task completion.

1	2	3	4	5
Never or Rarely	Occasionally	Sometimes	Frequently	Almost Always

☐ NA

7. Informs you of the project's progress or delays.

1	2	3	4	5
Never or Rarely	Occasionally	Sometimes	Frequently	Almost Always

☐ NA

8. Maintains a positive attitude.

1	2	3	4	5
Never or Rarely	Occasionally	Sometimes	Frequently	Almost Always

☐ NA

9. Consults with experts.

1	2	3	4	5
Never or Rarely	Occasionally	Sometimes	Frequently	Almost Always

☐ NA

10. Please describe what you see as this member's key contribution to the team:

Please return to Brenda in Human Resources by Friday, June 5.

Thanks again for your participation.

Mike was generally pleased . . .

with his own results on the Peer Report. His goal was to reach a 4.0 average on all the items. As you can see by the illustrated graph, he scored low on *"informing"* for the six internal customers and suppliers. Mike decided to ask the team for their suggestions on how he might improve in this area. . . .

Peer Feedback Survey Scores for Mike

ITEM	AVERAGE SCORE FROM OTHER TEAM MEMBERS	AVERAGE SCORE FROM INTERNAL CUSTOMER/ SUPPLIER GROUP
Focused on purpose and goals	5.0	4.5
Involves others in data collection	4.1	4.0
Delegates or requests help	4.6	4.7
Learns about needs and concerns of others	4.8	4.6
Open to suggestions	4.2	3.9
Keeps commitments on completion	4.4	4.6
Informs on progress or delays	3.9	2.9
Positive attitude	4.6	4.8
Consults with experts	4.3	3.2
AVERAGE ALL ITEMS	**4.4**	**4.1**

What others see as your key contributions:

- Appreciate sense of commitment
- Push for results keeps others motivated

Mike took immediate action . . .

by sending an E-mail update on the team's latest decisions to every department manager. Since *"consulting experts"* was his second lowest score, he wanted to solicit additional suggestions from each manager as well as offer them timely project updates. He planned to visit different department managers within the next two days.

At the end of the 90-day project, Mike's team repeated the survey. The results of the surveys made up 20 percent of each member's performance evaluation.

Guidelines for peer feedback

Here are guidelines to keep in mind when your team decides to use peer feedback as part of your measurement:

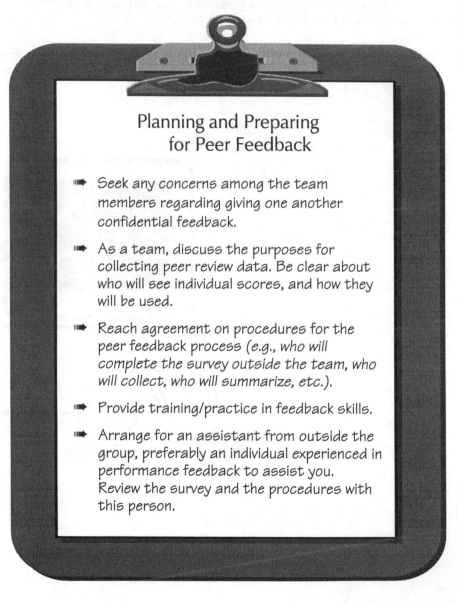

Planning and Preparing for Peer Feedback

➡ Seek any concerns among the team members regarding giving one another confidential feedback.

➡ As a team, discuss the purposes for collecting peer review data. Be clear about who will see individual scores, and how they will be used.

➡ Reach agreement on procedures for the peer feedback process (e.g., who will complete the survey outside the team, who will collect, who will summarize, etc.).

➡ Provide training/practice in feedback skills.

➡ Arrange for an assistant from outside the group, preferably an individual experienced in performance feedback to assist you. Review the survey and the procedures with this person.

Life after peer surveys

Your work is just beginning. Here's what you need to do after collecting completed surveys:

- Summarize results by source for individuals and the team as a whole.

- Prepare a summary of the group's average scores on each item.

- Confidentially distribute individual results to team members.

- Encourage individuals to identify several developmental tasks for themselves based on their results (individual action plans).

- As a team, plan to take action on any items where the group average was lower than acceptable.

Observation

The tool of observation, with its hundreds of variations, provides a *systematic* means for people to watch a team's actual performance in a work setting. However, the types of observations you use to measure performance are more structured and focused than a casual observation.

As Lee's team began to consider . . .

possible strategies for increasing their hotel's guest return rate, they asked a member of the marketing staff to observe their activities. Lee and his team members felt that a simple observation session could provide a starting point. Perhaps there were things they were doing or not doing that might make a difference to the guests. . . .

The team asked their observer-partner to listen and look for eight specific interactions on the part of the registration clerks. The team and the observer developed a check sheet to track team behavior.

Armed with his check sheet of items . . .

the observer was able to count the number of times each of the interactions happened. The agreement with Lee's team was to observe for three, 30-minute periods per day, for two days. They would stagger the observation schedule to cover peak registration periods. The marketing assistant dressed like a tourist to blend into the setting. . . .

Lee's Team's Observation Check Sheet

REGISTRATION DESK OBSERVATION CHECK SHEET

Observation Date and Time: Tues., May 2 5:15 - 5:45 P.M.
Number of Guests Observed: 17 parties registered during this period

BEHAVIOR/INTERACTION	NUMBER OF TIMES OBSERVED
Party waited five minutes or less for available registration clerk.	ⅢⅡ ⅢⅡ ⅢⅡ
Clerk uses the guest's name at least twice during the interaction?	ⅢⅡ ⅢⅡ ||||
Clerk makes eye contact with guest at least twice?	ⅢⅡ ⅢⅡ |||
Multiple guests in the party? Clerk makes effort to greet companions of guests?	ⅢⅡ ⅢⅡ | ⅢⅡ ⅢⅡ
Clerk is able to locate the guest's registration paperwork within one minute?	ⅢⅡ |||| **Note:** 2x, paperwork took longer than 3 minutes to locate.
Clerk confirms the guest's address, choice of room type, and length of stay?	ⅢⅡ ⅢⅡ ⅢⅡ ||
Credit card used? If so, card returned without the guest having to ask for it?	ⅢⅡ ⅢⅡ ⅢⅡ | ⅢⅡ ⅢⅡ ⅢⅡ |
Offers the desk's assistance for any of the guest's needs during his/her visit?	ⅢⅡ ⅢⅡ |||

For this measurement process, Lee's team was interested in the number of times interactions occurred—a quantitative measure. Often, observation can provide valuable qualitative data as well. A good observer can usually capture both kinds of information. This is discussed further in Chapter Six.

Plan your observations carefully. You should brief external observers on the procedures and specifics of what your team seeks. Their accuracy and objectivity is very important. Design check sheets for efficient note taking, and conduct a practice observation in advance of the real one.

Existing Data

Rather than duplicate data collection efforts, successful teams find and use data that already exists in their own departments or elsewhere in their organizations. Teams can find existing data in Human Resources, Finance, Sales, or Marketing departments. Occasionally, a supplier's organization or a customer will also have interesting performance data on your organization.

Some examples of existing quantitative data include:

- Quality assurance records
- Work-in-progress inventories
- Error-free orders
- Budgets-on-target
- On-time deliveries
- Sales records (noting increases or decreases)
- Vendor service ratings
- Previous lead times for new products
- Quality measures in each department
- Records of customer response times

- Organizational and departmental audits
- Project milestones
- Organizational and departmental customer surveys
- Employee opinion surveys
- Retention and turnover figures
- Sickness and absenteeism reports
- Logs of meetings to solve a particular problem/associated meeting costs
- Calendars and time logs
- Accident and workers' compensation costs

Let's look at how our three teams used existing data to track their performance.

Trina's Outpatient team was formed . . .

as a direct result of existing data. The hospital's most recent employee opinion survey revealed two low scores *(in comparison with the hospital average)* that surprised the group. These low scores were on the following two survey items:

> The people in my work group cooperate well with each other.
> The morale in my work group is good.

In addition to the annual employee survey, the hospital conducts quarterly patient satisfaction surveys. Looking at these results, Trina's team found that they scored *"Less Than Satisfactory"* on registration services and patient waiting times.

The quantitative data on both surveys served as a big *"wake-up call"* for the Outpatient Department and led to the formation of Trina's team to tackle the identified problems.

Existing data was also useful to . . .

Mike's new product team. The previous new product team's planning and milestone charts, as well as charts from the past four weeks plainly demonstrated inadequate scheduling performance.

From their organization's annual employee survey, the team learned that of all departments, the engineering department scored lowest on two items:

> Our department receives information about external customers.
> Our department receives information from internal customers.

Taking their cue from the data, the team made plans to increase communication between customers and engineers.

Lastly, Lee's registration desk team used . . .

several sources of existing data. The numbers of new and returning guests were readily available through the computer system. The Sales Department also had industry averages on returning guests for moderately priced hotels.

Although each team found and used existing quantitative data, they were also aware of the benefits of supplementing the numbers with qualitative data, as you will see in the next chapter.

SUMMARY

☑ In measurement, knowing how you plan to use the results will determine how you should obtain your data. If performance issues are sensitive and feelings are strong, observation will not work. Confidential surveys distributed by a third party are best in this situation. However, if the data you want to collect exists elsewhere, don't waste people's time by asking them to complete a survey.

☑ Quantitative measures give teams new targets to reach, and expose trouble spots for the team to correct. No one measurement tool works best in every circumstance; sometimes it is best to combine surveys, observations, and existing data.

☑ When we tune into a weather report, we need to know more than the air temperature. We need readings on the humidity, barometric pressure, and wind velocity to give us a complete weather picture. Each reading requires a different tool. Our three teams are familiar with the quantitative tools. For a clearer reading on performance, they want depth and detail to explain the numbers. Qualitative measures provide just that.

CHAPTER FIVE WORKSHEET:
GATHERING YOUR QUANTITATIVE DATA

1. What are the benefits and potential obstacles to using the Team Success Survey with your team?

BENEFITS	POTENTIAL OBSTACLES

2. What are the benefits and potential hurdles to using the Meeting Effectiveness Survey with your team?

BENEFITS	POTENTIAL OBSTACLES

3. What are the benefits and potential obstacles to using the Peer Feedback Survey with your team?

BENEFITS	POTENTIAL OBSTACLES

4. What elements will you include as you develop your survey(s)?

_____

_____

_____

5. Which scale(s) will you use?

_____

_____

_____

6. Which open-ended questions will you include?

_____

_____

_____

7. What specific opportunities does your team have to use Observation as a data gathering tool to measure team performance?

_____

_____

_____

_____

_____

_____

_____

_____

8. What existing data can be used more effectively to measure your team's performance?

_____

_____

_____

_____

_____

_____

_____

_____

QUALITATIVE MEASURES: THE POWER OF PERCEPTION

Star basketball players know where their team stands. On a daily basis, they have a grasp of specific statistics and quantitative data *(in this case, games won and games lost)*. This data tells them where they are relative to their objective—the championship. This data also gives those players a sense of the team's morale.

Qualitative data, whether positive or negative, complements the numbers and provides valuable feedback for teams. Some teams even appreciate complaints as *"treasures"* to mine.

You may have heard someone say, *"That is only the customer's perception."* Perceptions affect people's decisions to buy services, use a particular hospital, or invest in new products at the prototype stage. Qualitative measures help teams understand these perceptions and points of view.

Our teams use three kinds of qualitative measures to help them understand the numbers, make better decisions, and reach their goals. These tools are:

✔ Interviews

✔ Observation

✔ Critical Incidents

Interviews

Interviews are excellent sources of qualitative measurement. A good interviewer asks questions to discover people's needs, interests, concerns, opinions, or even fears and hopes surrounding a situation or issue. These interviews are usually conducted in private.

Group interviews gather opinions from several people at once. When the issues are complex or when you want to involve people in your team's work, interviewing is preferable to conducting surveys.

If your team is going to use interviews to obtain team performance feedback, consider the following guidelines before, during, and after the interviews:

Before the interviews

➡ Record the purpose for the interviews, and how you expect to use the information you collect.

➡ Determine key content areas and topics. Limit your topics to one or two. Draft several questions related to each area. Use open-ended questions as much as possible.

➡ Target your interviewees. Seek: persons who are affected by your work, service or processes; senior managers who have authority over your team's work, and experts and objective outsiders.

➡ Schedule the interviews. Explain the purpose of them. Confirm the time and place the day before.

➡ If you are not an experienced interviewer, practice the interview with a colleague—perhaps your note taker. Ask for feedback on your interviewing style.

During the interviews

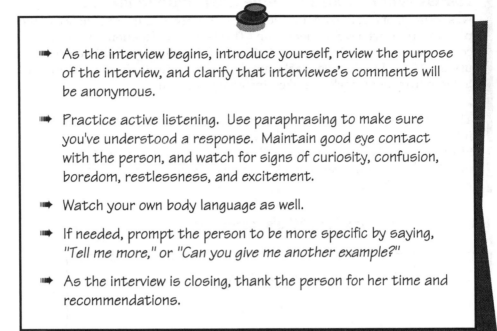

➡ As the interview begins, introduce yourself, review the purpose of the interview, and clarify that interviewee's comments will be anonymous.

➡ Practice active listening. Use paraphrasing to make sure you've understood a response. Maintain good eye contact with the person, and watch for signs of curiosity, confusion, boredom, restlessness, and excitement.

➡ Watch your own body language as well.

➡ If needed, prompt the person to be more specific by saying, *"Tell me more,"* or *"Can you give me another example?"*

➡ As the interview is closing, thank the person for her time and recommendations.

After the interviews

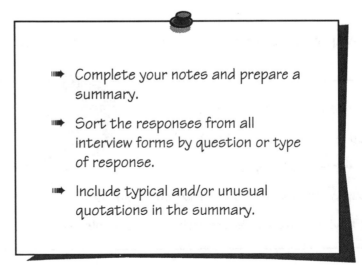

➡ Complete your notes and prepare a summary.

➡ Sort the responses from all interview forms by question or type of response.

➡ Include typical and/or unusual quotations in the summary.

When Mike's ski pole prototype team . . .

was formed, one of the organization's directors recalled the experience of the previous product development team. This team had experienced serious communication and cooperation problems. Since the organization planned to use this type of cross-functional team often in the future, she was determined to learn from everyone's mistakes, including her own.

The director asked Brenda *(from the organization's Human Resources office)* to interview members of the previous team and several members of Mike's team. She hoped that the qualitative data from these interviews would help Mike's new team and future teams break through the significant barriers the previous group met. . . .

Interview questions for Mike's team:

What do you see as your team's objective?

What can you contribute to your team?

Tell me about the things that are working well right now.

What are the barriers to your team's success?

How can you overcome these barriers?

Interview questions for members of the previous team:

What was your team's objective?

Do you feel you met the objective?

What worked well on your team?

What were the barriers that held your team back?

What advice would you share with Mike's ski pole team?

Brenda identified three themes . . .

in a brief summary for the director:

1. Day-to-day communication and the need to keep the members' respective departments informed

2. Planning assignments

3. The importance of recognizing individual contributions as well as the team effort. . . .

Observation

Observation offers qualitative data as well as quantitative data. A keen observer will notice and be able to describe the mood of an office. The observer will see the *"spirit"* displayed by the front desk staff, the frown on the guest's face, or the lack of focus during meetings of the new product development team.

Observation is such a straightforward approach to measurement that it is often overlooked. It works well when:

➥ It is important to study the actual work habits of the team.

➥ You need to see a comprehensive picture of the work environment: the roles, the movements of people and equipment, and the physical setting.

➥ There is no time for surveys and interviews, which are indirect and somewhat removed from the performance setting anyway.

➥ You need flexibility of measurement (*e.g., if the team knows there is a problem but does not yet understand it well enough to develop a survey*).

➥ Work is routine, repetitive, and perhaps, taken for granted.

During the observation, the observer is focused on what is happening rather than on his or her interpretation of why it is happening. Analysis and interpretation come later in the process.

The observation check sheet is the observer's key tool. Check sheets are simple tables, usually with blank columns and rows to record frequencies, counts, times, etc.

You may want to include a column to record notes about interactions and behaviors that cannot be counted or that influence the numbers in some way. You can use an *"activities key"* or list of abbreviations to make the note taking more efficient.

Trina's team agreed to gather some notes . .

on patient and staff activities to gain insight into possible causes of the long waits and schedule disruptions. Some of the patient activities the team wanted to note included seeking assistance from the receptionist (SA), filling out forms (FF), and reading (RD). Some of the staff activities included talking on the telephone (TT), looking for patient files (LF), and helping the patient fill out forms (HF). . . .

Here are excerpts from their *"Notes"* column:

NOTES

Patient A arrived early. Staff not aware pt was waiting until 15 min. after his arrival. Receptionist busy with another patient-he forgot insurance card and experienced other problems while FF.

Patient B arrived early, apparently was not clear on scheduled appointment time. Total wait time was 25 minutes *(officially)* but patient sat in office for 40 minutes.

Patient C is five minutes late and very agitated about missing appointment. Major problems with insurance forms. Approximately 15 minutes SA.

Patient D is 15 minutes late due to traffic. Because D is late, another patient takes her place.

Patient E is on time. Prep room back-up due to late patients.

Critical Incidents

Countless events occur in organizations every day that, if observed, recorded and summarized, would reveal patterns and trends in team performance. Critical incidents are the qualitative side of existing data, which was described in Chapter Five. They are a gold mine of information lying just below the surface in our files and memories. Most employees can recall stories *(sometimes spicy ones)* about this patient, that guest, or some customer.

Patterns and trends of critical incidents are useful to teams in two ways:

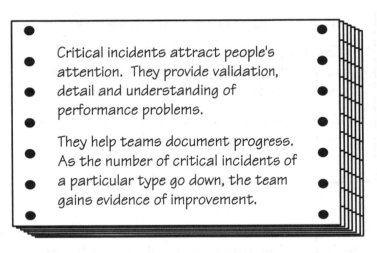

Critical incidents attract people's attention. They provide validation, detail and understanding of performance problems.

They help teams document progress. As the number of critical incidents of a particular type go down, the team gains evidence of improvement.

Examples of critical incidents include:

- Letters of appreciation
- Complaint letters or phone calls
- Incidences of excellent service

Smart teams are alert for critical incidents as indicators of problems. They actually seek them out by adding the following kinds of questions to surveys or face-to-face interviews:

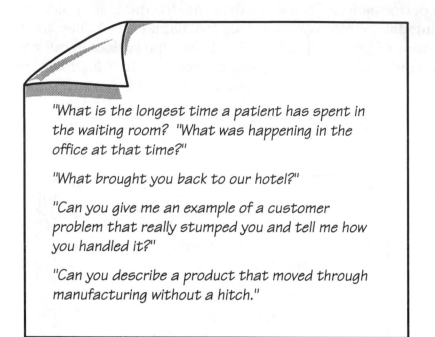

"What is the longest time a patient has spent in the waiting room? "What was happening in the office at that time?"

"What brought you back to our hotel?"

"Can you give me an example of a customer problem that really stumped you and tell me how you handled it?"

"Can you describe a product that moved through manufacturing without a hitch."

Summarizing the information from critical incidents is more complex than adding numbers or calculating the percentages involved in quantitative measurement, but it is well worth the time. However, unless you record critical incidents, they become war stories without the benefit of learning or action.

Trina's team used two critical incidents . . .

to improve their waiting room time. They studied a complaint letter from a patient who was forgotten in the waiting room and they discussed a telephone call from an angry physician. Both incidents were clear indicators of coordination problems among the outpatient department staff. These critical incidents, in combination with the observation check sheets, reinforced the need for improvement.

SUMMARY

☑ Qualitative data is an essential element of measuring for team performance. It supplements and deepens our understanding of quantitative measurements . . . and often provides information that numbers cannot. Qualitative measures have a way of opening our eyes to performance problems that require attention.

☑ Open-ended questions form the basis for interviews. They allow the interviewer to learn directly about the needs, concerns, ideas, and interests of people involved or affected by performance.

☑ Observation is underutilized as a qualitative measurement tool. With observations, we gain insights into good and problem performance. Such insight helps to explain frequencies, counts, times, and other quantitative measures.

☑ Critical incidents are drawn from data that departments or organizations collect or receive on an ongoing basis. With organization and focus, they can be used as important performance indicators.

CHAPTER SIX WORKSHEET:
GETTING BEHIND THE NUMBERS

1. What specific opportunities does your team have to conduct interviews and obtain team performance feedback?

_____

_____

2. For three of the situations you noted above, please answer the following questions:

a) Who will be interviewed?

_____

_____

b) Who will conduct the interviews?

_____

_____

c) What information will be obtained?

_____

_____

d) How and when will your team use the information?

_____

_____

3. What specific opportunities does your team have to use observation to gather qualitative team performance information?

_____

_____

4. For three of the situations you noted above, please answer the following questions:

a) Who will do the observing?

_____

_____

b) What briefing will be given to those being observed?

_____

_____

c) How will the information be interpreted and used by your team?

_____

_____

5. What specific opportunities does your team have to use critical incident monitoring?

_____

_____

6. How will your team gather and use the information for these critical incidents?

_____

_____

USING THE RESULTS

Arriving at the point where your team is ready to use the results of its measurements is an achievement in itself! It takes considerable time *(especially the first time)*, and some courage to identify performance concerns, develop tools, apply them, and summarize the results.

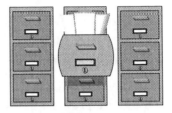

Now that you have your measurements, don't hide them in a file drawer.

Instead, your team can:

- Interpret Your Results

- Set New Goals

- Evaluate Your Performance

- Celebrate Your Success

Interpret Your Results

The survey scores and interview summaries are in front of you.
The team is seated around the table looking at you eagerly. What
do you do next? Here are the steps to take:

➡ Review the purpose of the measurement and how it
supports your team's mission.

➡ Help your team understand the scores, the number of
responses, and the scales, check sheets and other tools
that your team used.

➡ Put the measures in context. Compare numerical scores
to the team's baseline scores or organizational averages, if
they are available and relevant.

➡ Discuss the range. Point out the highest positive scores
and look at the lowest scores.

➡ As needed, maintain confidentiality.

➡ Using the qualitative data, discuss the reasons behind the
high and low scores.

➡ Explore the difficult results through open communication;
don't be afraid of healthy disagreement. Focus on the
group interest and common objectives.

➡ Prioritize the problem areas you want to address in the
meeting.

➡ Complete an action planning guide.

When Trina's team . . .

looked at their Team Success Survey scores for the first time, they were
discouraged and immediately wanted to blame the physicians and insurance
companies for several of their low scores. Alexis (*from Human Resources*)
helped the group stay focused on their role and responsibility for the
measures. . . .

Here are the results of Trina's Team's Success Survey:

ITEM	# OF RESP.	POINT RANGE	TOTAL POINTS	POINT AVERAGE	RANK (BY AVG.)
Clearly states mission/goals	7	4 - 6	34	4.9	4
Operates creatively	7	3 - 7	37	5.3	2
Focuses on results	7	4 - 5	31	4.3	6
Clarifies roles and responsibilities	7	2 - 6	34	4.9	4
Is well-organized	7	4 - 6	36	5.1	3
Builds upon individual strengths	7	5 - 7	41	5.9	1
Supports leadership/each other	7	4 - 6	37	5.3	2
Develops team climate	5	3 - 5	21	4.2	7
Resolves disagreements	6	2 - 5	20	3.3	9
Communicates openly	7	2 - 4	21	3.0	10
Makes objective decisions	7	3 - 6	33	4.7	5
Evaluates its own effectiveness	7	2 - 4	24	3.4	8

First, the team . . .

focused on their strengths. They were glad to see that their group did well, averaging 5.0 points or higher, in several areas.

Then the team took note of the two lowest scores, *(Resolves disagreements— 3.3)* and *(Communicates openly—3.0)*. Because these areas are so interrelated and together can block the team's progress on any of the other success factors, Trina's team decided to focus their efforts on them over the next four weeks. The team would simultaneously collect observation data on patient waiting times.

They also discussed the existing data from the organization's employee opinion survey. The team's low scores—compared to hospital averages—on coworker cooperation and morale further confirmed their need to take action. Lastly, the study of two critical incidents, a patient's complaint letter and an angry physician's phone call, underlined the urgency of their situation.

With Alexis' assistance, the team drafted several new ground rules to improve cooperation within the office. One rule was to write messages carefully. Another was to use a communication logbook so that detailed appointment and insurance information would not be lost. The team was wise to select just a few areas to correct. Attempting to fix every problem revealed by the measurements at the same time would have hindered their focus and led to certain failure. . . .

Set New Goals

Many teams make the mistake of analyzing, discussing, and defending their data without taking action. These teams are *"data rich and results poor."* Good action plans cover goals, time frames, resources, and a person who accepts responsibility for each task.

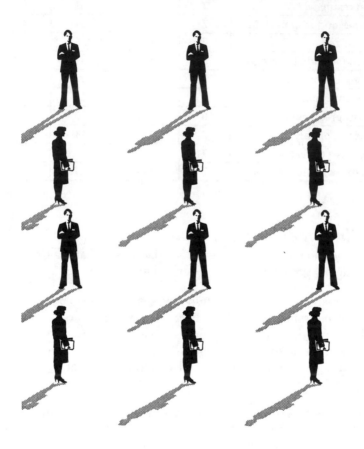

✠ *Everyone agreed . . .*

that for a four-week period, they would all follow the new ground rules. They scheduled a review meeting at the end of the four weeks to assess progress and make other adjustments as needed. The team decided to repeat the Team Success Survey every month *(for several months at least)* and to discuss and review their ground rules. . . .

They created the following realistic action plan.

Name: Outpatient Department

Goal Statement: To reduce patient waiting time by 50% while maintaining a 90 percent rating on customer satisfaction

ACTION STEPS:	PERSON(S) RESPONSIBLE	DATES AND TIMES
Note all written and verbal messages carefully	All	Immediate
Use a communication logbook daily	All	Immediate
Request that new patients arrive 20 minutes early to complete insurance paperwork; returning patients 10 minutes early	Trina and John	Immediate
Follow through on tasks and ask for help when needed	All	Immediate
Attend an effective meetings workshop	All	3/8
Hold weekly meetings to work on 50% reduction goal	All	Begin 4/16

MEASURES OR PROGRESS REPORTS	OBSTACLES TO BE OVERCOME	AVAILABLE RESOURCES
Team Success Survey/Monthly 10% increase	Taking time for weekly meetings	Receptionist from lab will cover phones
Employee Opinion Survey items/10% increase	Dislike of meetings	Temporary: Two one-hour block-out periods for patient appointments per month (*probably Friday P.M.*)
Use Meeting Effectiveness Survey tool	Loss of initial momentum	
Review/Discuss Observation notes		

Evaluate Your Performance

The Outpatient Team worked hard over several months to build trust and communication. They began taking the Team Success Survey every month *(adding specific questions on the two targeted areas)*. This enabled them to remove the barriers that affected patient waiting times.

With the approval of the hospital's Assistant Administrator, the team negotiated alternate performance measures for their annual performance evaluations. A portion of everyone's review would now be based on:

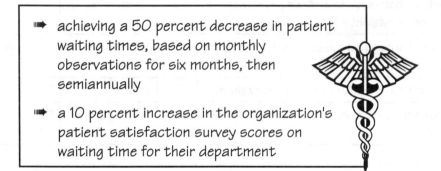

> ➡ achieving a 50 percent decrease in patient waiting times, based on monthly observations for six months, then semiannually
>
> ➡ a 10 percent increase in the organization's patient satisfaction survey scores on waiting time for their department

Celebrate Your Success

Strong teams continuously learn how to use measures as a basis for goal setting and action.

One reason to measure team performance is to motivate your team. Recognizing your team's accomplishment of its goals is a key to using measurement as a motivator.

When teams set important business goals that they can influence and control, and when progress toward these goals is measured fairly and carefully, the team deserves rewards.

▼ *After three months . . .*

Trina's team noticed definite improvements when they compared the new scores to baseline data. They enjoyed their accomplishments and posted their monthly scores as large red numbers. Trina's group celebrated with a team breakfast sponsored by the Assistant Administrator at an exclusive restaurant near the hospital. . . .

Let's review some tips for using your results:

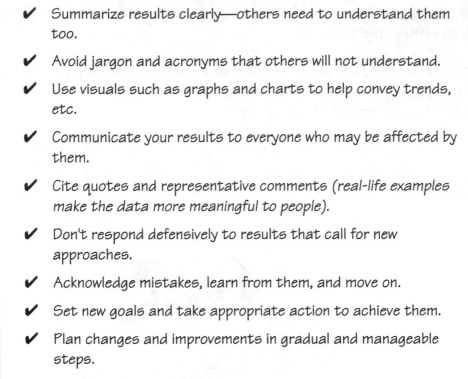

> ✔ Summarize results clearly—others need to understand them too.
>
> ✔ Avoid jargon and acronyms that others will not understand.
>
> ✔ Use visuals such as graphs and charts to help convey trends, etc.
>
> ✔ Communicate your results to everyone who may be affected by them.
>
> ✔ Cite quotes and representative comments (real-life examples make the data more meaningful to people).
>
> ✔ Don't respond defensively to results that call for new approaches.
>
> ✔ Acknowledge mistakes, learn from them, and move on.
>
> ✔ Set new goals and take appropriate action to achieve them.
>
> ✔ Plan changes and improvements in gradual and manageable steps.
>
> ✔ Celebrate your successes!

CHAPTER SEVEN WORKSHEET:
USING YOUR MEASUREMENT INFORMATION

1. Who will be involved in the interpretation of your team's performance measurement information?

_____

_____

_____

2. How will decisions be made about which key team performance areas to focus on? *(e.g., team decision, team leader decision, etc.)*

_____

_____

_____

3. How will the results be tied to your formal performance evaluation process?

_____

_____

4. How will your team celebrate its accomplishments?

_____

_____

_____

CHAPTER EIGHT

SUMMARY

Measures serve as rallying points and motivators for teams. Successful teams plan what to measure and how to measure, and they act on the results.

Measuring Team Performance introduced three work teams; each with different business objectives, and each having a different experience level as a team. Measurement was beneficial for all three teams. They designed custom tools to help them meet their business objectives.

To measure effectively, measure what matters. Be aware of your team's needs from two perspectives. First, know your business objectives. If your team is service-oriented like Trina's or Lee's, your measures of success relate to things like patient satisfaction or return hotel guests. A product team such as Mike's will measure their success by a calendar and a budget—in this case, a workable prototype by June 1st that can be manufactured at a cost under ten dollars.

Second, never forget your team's dynamics and communication—the factors that help or hinder your team from moving toward your objective. Teams that pay little or no attention to their internal workings are more likely to fail than teams that do.

Guidelines for the art of measurement

Introduce measurement gradually

Begin with something simple, or something internal to the team. For example, start with a 10-item point of service survey rather than in-depth interviews with 20 critical customers. If needed, help members of the team become more comfortable by offering training in delivering and receiving feedback as a team. Team leaders and facilitators can model effective feedback skills by asking for feedback on their own performance, and responding with appreciation.

Use three or four essential measures

Keep the practice of measurement in perspective; it is a means to an end. Three or four tools, strategically applied, should serve your team's needs.

Address teamwork

Develop a measurement plan that addresses each major teamwork category: Results, Team Dynamics, and Team Communication. The Team Success Survey is an example of a tool that incorporates all three categories in one survey. Depending on the needs of the team, other tools may focus on just one of the categories. Strive for improvement.

Use a 360-degree survey

Consider multiple sources of input: the team itself, the team's internal suppliers and customers, the organization's customers *(if the team has contact with them);* the organization's senior management; and facilitators or trainers.

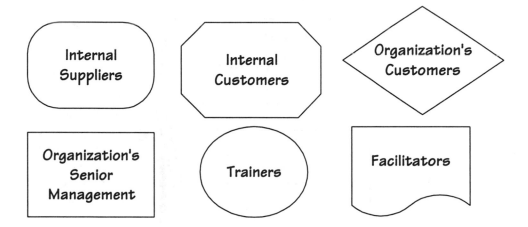

Use various tools, both quantitative and qualitative

Together the two kinds provide a more complete picture than either can independently. When appropriate, combine quantitative and qualitative measures within the same tool. Examples of this include a survey that uses several open-ended questions, or an observation check sheet with space for notes.

Measure the right things

You need to know both where you're going and how you're going to get there. The right things to measure are: the milestones and results that deal with your team's business objective; and the structures and teamwork behaviors that lead to the objective. Connect the measures to what you want to reinforce. Remember that what gets measured gets learned, becomes habit, and gets done.

Measure often

Use a short, easy-to-complete meeting effectiveness questionnaire. Comment on improvements and changes in meeting productivity at every meeting. Merely asking members to complete the questionnaire once every six months would not result in more effective team meetings.

Keep it simple

Developing measures is a creative process. Once people accept the idea of measurement, there is a tendency to overmeasure, or conduct measures at an unnecessary level of detail. In most cases, three or four short, strategic, simple tools will work far better than one elaborate measurement tool that is cumbersome to take and analyze.

Share the responsibility for measurement among team members

Some team tasks are assigned to certain individuals because they possess the specific skills (*or speed, or experience*) to accomplish them. The development, administration and interpretation of team measures requires a clear sense of purpose, some common sense, the ability to organize information, and reasonably good communication skills. These skills exist in most teams, so take advantage of them.

Make your findings understandable; then communicate them

Visual tools such as bar charts, summary data tables, Pareto diagrams and pie charts are generally more effective than words alone. Don't give people pages of computer numbers and printouts filled with means and scores.

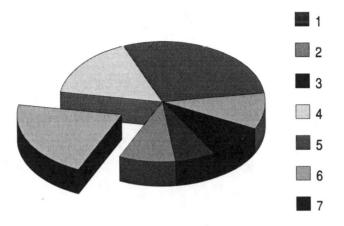

Discuss and evaluate your findings

It takes courage for a team to evaluate their own work; even more to ask others to provide feedback. However, this becomes easier with some measurement experience.

When reviewing the results, your group's silence does not mean that everyone understands the information. Discuss the purpose and use of the data. Take time to establish priorities, define actions, set time frames and select assignments. Make the measurement process meaningful.

Take action on the results

When something positive and constructive happens as a result of a measurement, people notice. Action—especially improvement—helps people feel good about the measurement process and motivates them to continue it.

SPECIAL SITUATIONS

Check any of the following that apply to your team's situation:

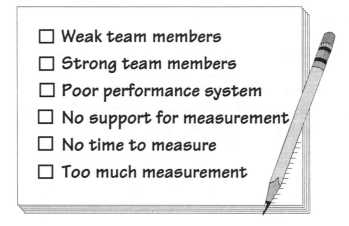

☐ Weak team members
☐ Strong team members
☐ Poor performance system
☐ No support for measurement
☐ No time to measure
☐ Too much measurement

These are many special situations or challenges that arise when teams decide to measure their performance. A few cautions and suggestions will help your team plan for them.

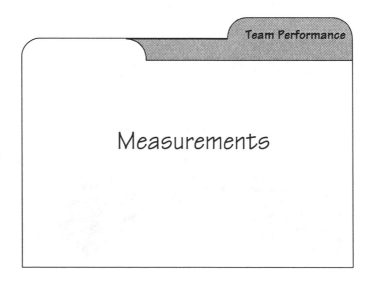

Team Performance

Measurements

☒ Issue: Weak team members

With hard work and effort, a particular team achieves their business goals and receives a financial bonus. Later, they discover that one member of the five-person team performed very little actual work. The team members grow increasingly resentful.

Suggestions:

➡ Measure the team's effectiveness using the Team Success Survey at regular intervals. Address low scores. See that roles and responsibilities are clear. Each team member should understand what is expected of him or her. Pay attention to conflict over uneven performance. You may ask for an outside facilitator to assist you.

➡ Build peer and 360-degree feedback into your measurement plan. Consider a mid-project peer review (as Mike's team did), so that members can make improvements before the end of the measuring period.

➡ Ask the Human Resources department to design a reward system that balances team and individual rewards. For example, base 25 percent of the reward system on individual team participation, using the 360-degree survey as your objective measure.

➡ Never let resentments and conflicts boil over.

➡ Tell weak members that you really need their help.

➡ Revisit your ground rules on handling poor performance.

➡ If all of the above fails, begin corrective action with the assistance of the Human Resources department.

⊠ Issue: Strong team members

One member hits the grand-slam home run that makes the difference between the team's success and failure on a critical project deadline. This person is the team's Most Valuable Player.

Suggestions:

➡ Ask the Human Resources department to design a reward system that balances team and individual rewards. For example, base 25 percent of the reward system on individual team participation using the 360-degree system as your objective measure.

➡ Assess, recognize and thank members for their unique contributions. You can ask an open-ended question on the Team Success Survey, such as: *"Describe any noteworthy individual contributions made by members of this team."*

➡ Arrange for public recognition of stellar performance and allow individuals an opportunity to praise their coworkers for the record.

⊠ Issue: Poor Performance System

An organization's traditional performance measurement system is based on individual contributions. There is no clear connection between team measures of performance and the compensation and reward system. Reviews are late and not very helpful.

Suggestions:

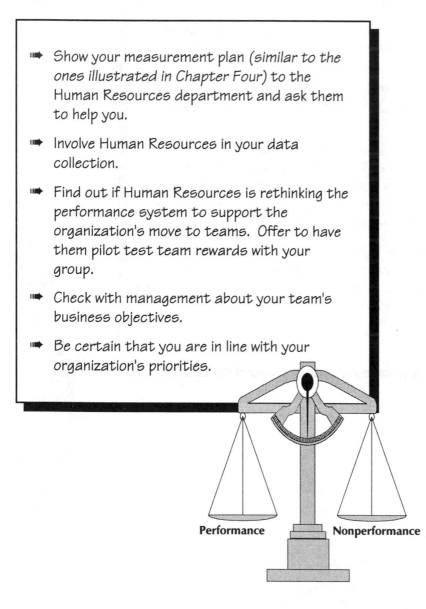

- Show your measurement plan (similar to the ones illustrated in Chapter Four) to the Human Resources department and ask them to help you.

- Involve Human Resources in your data collection.

- Find out if Human Resources is rethinking the performance system to support the organization's move to teams. Offer to have them pilot test team rewards with your group.

- Check with management about your team's business objectives.

- Be certain that you are in line with your organization's priorities.

Performance   Nonperformance

⊠ Issue: No support for measurement

During a series of observations, a team runs into a wall of resistance from other organizational teams and departments that are not cooperative.

Suggestions:

➠ Communicate your measurement plan. Involve the other departments and individuals early in the process.

➠ Focus on organizational goals.

➠ Ask departments about their experience with measurement. Try to understand their resistance.

➠ Be flexible. If your organization dislikes surveys, try observation.

➠ Use existing data and critical incidents the first year.

➠ Share your results with other groups and focus on what you learned and what you would do differently in the future.

➠ Post your results.

☒ Issue: No time to measure

One busy team waits until two weeks before the yearly performance evaluation season and discovers they don't have enough time to plan, conduct, and summarize their measurement in a way that can be used for the performance review.

Suggestions:

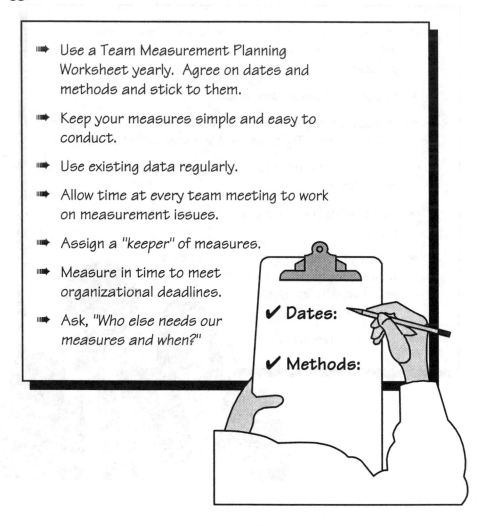

- Use a Team Measurement Planning Worksheet yearly. Agree on dates and methods and stick to them.

- Keep your measures simple and easy to conduct.

- Use existing data regularly.

- Allow time at every team meeting to work on measurement issues.

- Assign a "keeper" of measures.

- Measure in time to meet organizational deadlines.

- Ask, "Who else needs our measures and when?"

✔ Dates:

✔ Methods:

⊠ Issue: Too much measurement

One hospital dietary department uses more than 16 different surveys and/or interviews. Some surveys are 10 years old. This department is *"data rich and results poor."*

Suggestions:

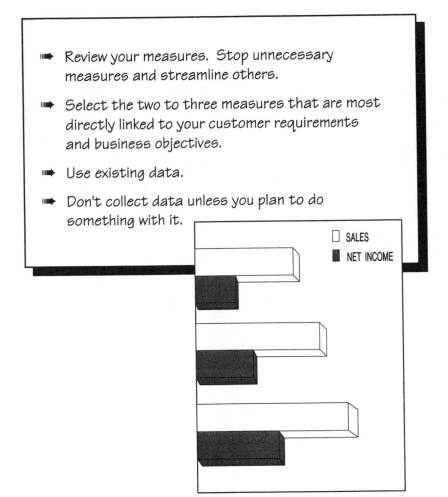

➠ Review your measures. Stop unnecessary measures and streamline others.

➠ Select the two to three measures that are most directly linked to your customer requirements and business objectives.

➠ Use existing data.

➠ Don't collect data unless you plan to do something with it.

☐ SALES
■ NET INCOME

REPRODUCIBLE FORMS

The following forms are provided for you to photocopy and use appropriately.

TEAM MEASUREMENT DECISION CHECKLIST

❏ We agree on the purpose of this measure *(tracking business goals, improving effectiveness, motivating, or evaluating performance for compensation)*

❏ We agree on measure's frequency *(daily, weekly, monthly, yearly)*

❏ We agree on the type of measurement *(survey, existing data, observation, interviews, critical incidents, etc.)*

❏ We agree on the questions to ask on the survey, interview or observation form.

❏ We agree on who will measure us *(team members, facilitator, management, suppliers, internal or external customers, etc.)*

❏ We agree on the administrative details of the measurement *(confidentiality, scoring, and distribution of results, etc.)*

❏ We will review the data on *(date)* to study the results, note improvements, analyze the causes of performance shortfalls, and take corrective action.

TEAM MEASUREMENT PLANNING WORKSHEET

Team's Business Objective:

▲Denotes a key measure for performance evaluation

TYPE OF MEASURE	WHO TO CONDUCT	SOURCES	TIMES/ FREQUENCY	NOTES

TEAM SUCCESS SURVEY

Name:_____ Team:_____ Date:_____

Please circle the number on each scale that you feel is most descriptive of your perception, as it relates to each item.

1. Clearly states its mission and goals

1	2	3	4	5	6	7

Team activities demonstrate a lack of focus or understanding of the team's mission and goals.

Team activities demonstrate a clear focus and understanding of the team's mission and goals.

2. Operates creatively

1	2	3	4	5	6	7

The team is unwilling to experiment with new ideas or methods.

The team experiments with new ideas and demonstrates a creative approach.

3. Focuses on results

1	2	3	4	5	6	7

The team does not accomplish its objectives within budget, on schedule, or to the required level of quality.

The team accomplishes its objectives within budget, on schedule and to the required level of quality.

4. Clarifies roles and responsibilities

1	2	3	4	5	6	7

Roles and responsibilities of team members are uncertain.

Roles and responsibilities are clear. Each team member understands what is expected of him or her.

5. Is well-organized

1	2	3	4	5	6	7

The team's structure, policies and procedures are disorganized.

The team's structure, policies and procedures are supported by its members.

6. Builds upon individual strengths

1	2	3	4	5	6	7

The knowledge, skills and talents of team members are underutilized.

Members' knowledge, skills and talents are put to good use.

7. Supports leadership and each other

1	2	3	4	5	6	7
The leadership role is always in the hands of one or two members. Others do not support the leadership.					The leadership role is shared among and supported by the team.	

8. Develops team climate

1	2	3	4	5	6	7
Team members feel they would be better off working individually.					Team members work together with a high degree of energy and involvement. There is a strong sense of team spirit.	

9. Resolves disagreements

1	2	3	4	5	6	7
Disagreement among team members interferes with productive work.					Members deal with disagreement openly and constructively.	

10. Communicates openly

1	2	3	4	5	6	7
Day-to-day communication among team members is limited and guarded.					Day-to-day communication among team members is frequent, honest, and direct.	

11. Makes objective decisions

1	2	3	4	5	6	7
Someone solves problems and makes decisions for the team.					The team identifies and solves its own problems, and makes effective decisions through involvement and consensus.	

12. Evaluates its own effectiveness

1	2	3	4	5	6	7
The team does not evaluate its own effectiveness.					The team continuously evaluates the effectiveness of its dynamics, methods, and performance.	

MEETING EFFECTIVENESS SURVEY

Name:_____ **Team:**_____ **Date:**_____

Please circle the number on each scale that you feel is most descriptive of your perception, as it relates to each item.

1. Did participants receive sufficient notice to prepare for this meeting?

0	1	2
No time	Some time	Sufficient time

2. Did the meeting notice or announcement include the purpose and objectives of the meeting?

0	1	2
Not indicated	Stated but unclear	Clearly stated

3. Did the meeting begin within three minutes of its scheduled start time?

0	1	2
No	Yes, but we had to start again for late arrivals	Yes

4. Was an agenda for the meeting prepared in advance, or developed at the start of the meeting?

0	1	2
No agenda/No stated objectives	Vague agenda and objectives	Specific agenda and clear objectives

5. At the beginning of the meeting, were the agenda (*including time lines for the topics*) and meeting objectives reviewed by the meeting leader or facilitator?

0	1	2
No	Yes, but not covered adequately	Yes

6. Were participants prepared for this meeting?

0	1	2
Not at all prepared	Somewhat prepared	As prepared as possible

7. Were action items and responsibilities clearly defined, then summarized?

0	1	2
Not at all	Some were/Others fuzzy	Yes

8. I would rate the quality of the group's interaction and member participation during this meeting as:

0	1	2
Having very little value	Fair	Very good/Contributed in a major way to effectiveness

9. Did the meeting generally follow the agenda and achieve its intended purpose?

0	1	2
Did not follow agenda	Followed the agenda somewhat	Followed the agenda in a productive manner

10. Did the meeting end within three minutes of its scheduled completion time, or sooner if business was accomplished?

0	1	2
No	No, but within a reasonable time frame	Yes

11. Overall, how did you feel about the investment of your time in this meeting?

0	1	2
Not at all satisfied/Frustrated	Somewhat satisfied	Completely satisfied/Something was accomplished/A good use of my time

Peer Feedback Survey

Name:_____ Team:_____ Date:_____

Rating Scale *(used in the Peer Feedback Survey)*

1. Never or Rarely *(less than 10% of the time)*
2. Occasionally *(about 10 to 30% of the time)*
3. Sometimes *(about 30 to 50% of the time)*
4. Frequently *(about 50 to 80% of the time)*
5. Almost always *(more than 80% of the time)*
   NA—Does not apply

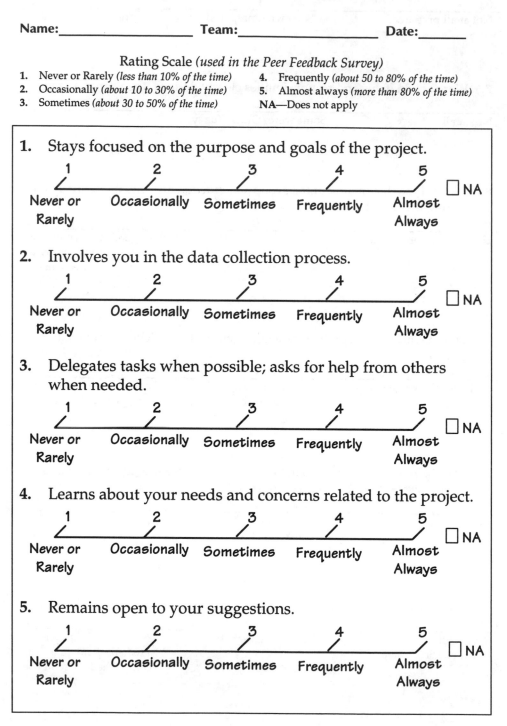

1. Stays focused on the purpose and goals of the project.

   | 1 | 2 | 3 | 4 | 5 |

   Never or / Occasionally / Sometimes / Frequently / Almost
   Rarely / / / / Always ☐ NA

2. Involves you in the data collection process.

   | 1 | 2 | 3 | 4 | 5 |

   Never or / Occasionally / Sometimes / Frequently / Almost
   Rarely / / / / Always ☐ NA

3. Delegates tasks when possible; asks for help from others when needed.

   | 1 | 2 | 3 | 4 | 5 |

   Never or / Occasionally / Sometimes / Frequently / Almost
   Rarely / / / / Always ☐ NA

4. Learns about your needs and concerns related to the project.

   | 1 | 2 | 3 | 4 | 5 |

   Never or / Occasionally / Sometimes / Frequently / Almost
   Rarely / / / / Always ☐ NA

5. Remains open to your suggestions.

   | 1 | 2 | 3 | 4 | 5 |

   Never or / Occasionally / Sometimes / Frequently / Almost
   Rarely / / / / Always ☐ NA

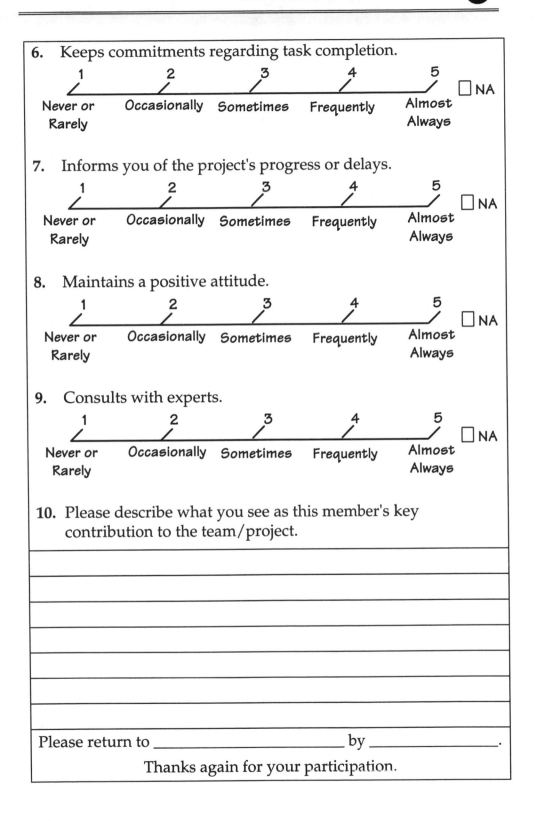

6. Keeps commitments regarding task completion.

1	2	3	4	5	☐ NA
Never or Rarely	Occasionally	Sometimes	Frequently	Almost Always	

7. Informs you of the project's progress or delays.

1	2	3	4	5	☐ NA
Never or Rarely	Occasionally	Sometimes	Frequently	Almost Always	

8. Maintains a positive attitude.

1	2	3	4	5	☐ NA
Never or Rarely	Occasionally	Sometimes	Frequently	Almost Always	

9. Consults with experts.

1	2	3	4	5	☐ NA
Never or Rarely	Occasionally	Sometimes	Frequently	Almost Always	

10. Please describe what you see as this member's key contribution to the team/project.

_____

_____

_____

_____

_____

_____

_____

Please return to _____ by _____.

Thanks again for your participation.

The Practical Guidebook Collection

Quality Improvement Series

- Meetings That Work!
- Continuous Improvement Tools Volume 1
- Continuous Improvement Tools Volume 2
- Step-By-Step Problem Solving
- Satisfying Internal Customers First!
- Continuous Process Improvement
- Improving Through Benchmarking
- Succeeding As A Self-Managed Team
- Reengineering In Action

Management Skills Series

- Coaching Through Effective Feedback
- Expanding Leadership Impact
- Mastering Change Management
- Effective Induction And Training
- Re-Creating Teams During Transitions

High Performance Team Series

- Success Through Teamwork
- Team Decision-Making Techniques
- Measuring Team Performance
- Building A Dynamic Team

High-Impact Training Series

- Creating High-Impact Training
- Identifying Targeted Training Needs
- Mapping A Winning Training Approach
- Producing High-Impact Learning Tools
- Applying Successful Training Techniques
- Measuring The Impact Of Training
- Make Your Training Results Last

EVALUATION AND FEEDBACK FORM

We need your help to continuously improve the quality of the resources provided through the Richard Chang Associates, Inc., Publications Division. We would greatly appreciate your input and suggestions regarding this particular guidebook, as well as future guidebook interests.

Please photocopy this form before completing it, since other readers may use this guidebook. Thank you in advance for your feedback.

Guidebook Title: _____

1. Overall, how would you rate your *level of satisfaction* with this guidebook? Please circle your response.

   Extremely Dissatisfied   Satisfied   Extremely Satisfied

        1   2   3   4   5

2. What specific *concepts or methods* did you find <u>most</u> helpful?

   _____
   _____

3. What specific *concepts or methods* did you find <u>least</u> helpful?

   _____
   _____

4. As an individual who may purchase additional guidebooks in the future, what *characteristics/features/benefits* are most important to you in making a decision to purchase a guidebook *(or another similar book)*?

   _____
   _____

5. What additional *subject matter/topic areas* would you like to see addressed in future guidebooks?

   _____
   _____

Name *(optional):* _____

Address: _____

C/S/Z: _____ **Phone (**   **)** _____

PLEASE FAX YOUR RESPONSES TO: (714) 756-0853 USA
OR (0171) 837-6348 UK